# Liza Minnelli Biography

A Life in Music and Hollywood

Boyce M. Dunphy

# COPYRIGHT PAGE

**Copyright © Boyce M. Dunphy, 2025.**

All rights reserved. No part of this publication may be reproduced, distributed, or transmitted in any form or by any means, including photocopying, recording, or other electronic or mechanical methods, without the prior written permission of the publisher, except in the case of brief quotations embodied in critical reviews and certain other noncommercial uses permitted by copyright law.

This book is an independent biography and is not authorized, endorsed, licensed, or affiliated with Liza Minnelli or any of his representatives. It is intended for informational and educational purposes only.

All trademarks and names mentioned belong to their respective owners and are used under fair use for descriptive purposes.

# TABLE OF CONTENT

COPYRIGHT PAGE..................................................1

INTRODUCTION....................................................4

CHAPTER ONE.......................................................7

   Early Life and Education....................................7

CHAPTER TWO....................................................14

   Rising Star in New York....................................14

CHAPTER THREE................................................18

   Liza Minnelli's Theatre.....................................18

CHAPTER FOUR..................................................24

   Liza Minnelli's Music........................................24

CHAPTER FIVE....................................................30

   Film.......................................................................30

CHAPTER SIX......................................................36

   Liza's Early TV Appearances and Variety Shows................................................................36

CHAPTER SEVEN...............................................41

Liza's Health Struggles and Impact on Performances .......................................................... 41
CHAPTER EIGHT ................................................... 47
   Personal Life of Liza Minnelli .......................... 47
CHAPTER NINE ...................................................... 55
   Philanthropy .................................................... 55
CONCLUSION ......................................................... 62

# INTRODUCTION

The name Liza Minnelli resonates across the heart of American culture like a timeless melody. Her captivating looks and powerful voice have left an indelible mark on the theater, film, and music industries from the day she first appeared on stage. Liza was bound for stardom, having been born into the bright legacy of Vincente Minnelli and Judy Garland, yet her journey has been incredible. She didn't only carry on her family's tradition; she pioneered the road and blazed trails that would forever change popular culture.

She began her career as a young girl with loftier ambitions than any Broadway stage, but her persistent passion, perseverance, and natural talent propelled her to worldwide stardom. Liza has constantly captivated audiences with her flawless alto voice, compelling stage presence, and ability to leave a piece of her soul in each performance, from her renowned depiction of Sally

Bowles in Cabaret to her legendary Carnegie Hall concerts.

This biography tries to portray aspects of Liza Minnelli's life, such as her joys, challenges, successes, and unbreakable spirit, in addition to recounting major events in her profession. Behind every song, dance, and scene in show business, there is a woman whose story is woven into the fabric. Liza's journey has been as wide and multifaceted as the roles she has portrayed, including marriages, health challenges, and reinventions.

As we dive into Liza Minnelli's story, we uncover more than just her career as a performer; we witness the heart and soul of a woman who has lasted the test of time and inspired generations via her songs, memories, and experiences. This book celebrates her time in Hollywood as well as music.

Join me as we examine the life of Liza Minnelli, a legend whose story is as colorful and interesting as the music she made.

# PART ONE
## Birth and Family Background

# CHAPTER ONE

## Early Life and Education

Liza May Minnelli was born on March 12, 1946, in Los Angeles, California, to two of Hollywood's most prominent figures: actress and singer Judy Garland and acclaimed filmmaker Vincente Minnelli. Liza has been immersed in the enchantment of the show industry since she was born. Her birth marked the beginning of a legacy that would go down in entertainment history. Liza, the daughter of such renowned personalities, seemed destined for the stage, but her tale would be molded by much more than her famous parents.

Judy Garland, best remembered for her portrayal as Dorothy in The Wizard of Oz, was a popular actress and singer during her time. Her strong voice and terrible personal life captivated millions of hearts, but she was also a woman dealing with the weight of fame, addiction, and mental distress. Vincente Minnelli, a talented filmmaker best remembered for his work on classic films like Meet Me in St. Louis and An American in Paris, was the creative force behind many of Hollywood's most famous musicals. They created a dynamic duo that epitomized the dazzling glamor and sometimes sad intricacies of Hollywood's golden age.

Despite their larger-than-life personalities, Liza's parents were profoundly influenced by the strains of celebrity. Judy, her mother, had a difficult work and personal life, including many marriages and struggles with addiction. Liza's father, Vincente, was an extremely gifted guy who was often gone owing to his busy job. Though their professional achievements were honored, Liza grew up in a household molded by their personal problems and emotional weight.

**Childhood and Early Influences**
Liza's early years were far from average. Growing up in a culture of splendor and public scrutiny, she was surrounded by great individuals from a young age. The Minnelli family was alive with music, theater, and the

buzz of Hollywood life. Her parents' lives were a mix of luxury and instability, as they were often preoccupied with their struggles, despite their wealth.

Liza was drawn to music and performing from an early age. Her mother, Judy Garland, had a powerful influence, her voice reverberating in Liza's ears since she was a kid. Judy's rehearsals and recordings formed the soundtrack of Liza's youth, revealing the power of music and narrative. Liza admired her mother much, and she was attracted to Judy's unwavering energy and ability to connect with an audience. Liza's early recollections did, however, contain some painful scenes as she witnessed her mother struggle with her inner turmoil.

Despite the difficulties of growing up in the shadow of such great personalities, Liza's early exposure to the entertainment industry kindled a flame in her. Her first steps on stage were when she was a youngster, performing for friends and family at the request of her mother. However, it was her inherent desire for the limelight, mixed with a great love of performing, that distinguished her.

**The Impact of Judy Garland and Vincente Minnelli**

Liza Minnelli's career was preordained as the daughter of two towering titans in showbiz. However, the unusual blend of influences from her parents shaped the woman she would become. Liza found inspiration in Judy Garland's larger-than-life presence, which demonstrated the wonder and force of performing. Liza inherited Judy's skill for commanding an audience and passionately investing herself in every song. Liza's mother's dedication to her profession and determination to devote herself entirely to her art served as an inspiration for her performances.

In contrast, Liza's father, Vincente Minnelli, taught her a distinct set of teachings. Vincente, a filmmaker recognized for his attention to detail, craftsmanship, and visual narrative, had an equally deep, if less obvious, impact on Liza. Liza grew up seeing her father's commitment to bringing large, sometimes extravagant, musicals to life. His skill to combine narrative and visual spectacle would subsequently be used in Liza's concerts, where every movement and gesture was as meticulously choreographed as the music she sang.

Perhaps most critically, the combination of Judy's emotional expressiveness and Vincente's visual creativity prepared Liza to flourish in both the musical and theatrical realms. Her ability to represent complex characters with emotional depth was influenced by her mother's heritage, but her painstaking attention to staging and movement reflected her father's influence. These early inspirations helped Liza Minnelli become one of her generation's most compelling and diverse performers.

Liza's upbringing was not without challenges, but it laid the groundwork for her to become one of the most vibrant and revered figures in entertainment. Surrounded by the glitz of Hollywood and her parents' distinct, sometimes volatile world, she discovered her voice and a love for acting, which would take her through decades of victories, tribulations, and memorable moments on stage and in film.

# PART TWO
## Moving to New York City

# CHAPTER TWO

## Rising Star in New York

Liza Minnelli made a daring choice in the early 1960s that would set the stage for her transforming path in the entertainment industry: she relocated to New York City. At the age of 16, she left the flashy but confusing world of Hollywood to forge her own identity in the city known for Broadway, jazz, and creative reinvention.

Liza's arrival in New York was more than simply a physical migration; it was a watershed moment in her personal and professional life. While she was born into the Hollywood spotlight, New York provided her with the opportunity to find her voice and pursue her passions outside of the shadow of her famous parents. The city, vibrant and full of energy, was ideal for a young woman eager to establish herself not only as the daughter of Judy Garland and Vincente Minnelli but also as a performer in her own right.

Her first days in the city were filled with both excitement and trepidation. Liza, who grew up with a strong musical and theatrical background, was determined to carve her career in the entertainment industry. New York, with its vibrant cultural environment, provided her with limitless opportunities. The city would eventually provide the background for her creative development, paving the way for her journey to success.

**First Steps in Show Business**

Liza Minnelli's debut into the world of show business was not simple, despite her family name. She quickly realized that success in the industry required more than just a well-known surname—talent, perseverance, and an undeniable stage presence. Despite her family's celebrity, Liza was initially determined to succeed on her own merits rather than relying solely on her parents' legacies.

Her first foray into show business was when she started performing in nightclubs and cabaret venues, honing her skills as a singer and performer. Liza's innate charm and raw skill rapidly drew the attention of the New York theatrical community. It wasn't long before she landed her first Broadway role, a watershed moment in her fledgling career. Her performance was full of the emotional depth and energy that she would come to be known for, and the audience took notice quickly.

Liza's early experiences in the nightclub and cabaret circuits helped her learn how to interact with an audience, which would later define her stage performances. These early years also taught her the art of musical storytelling, which she would later hone in her Broadway and film performances. Liza was more than just a talented performer; she was a rising star, ready to shine under the bright lights of Broadway.

# PART THREE

## Best Foot Forward (1963) and Broadway Beginnings

# CHAPTER THREE

## Liza Minnelli's Theatre

Liza Minnelli began her Broadway career at an early age, with the Off-Broadway production of Best Foot Forward in 1963. This early foray into the realm of live performance was more than simply a stepping stone; it was a watershed point in Liza's road to becoming a force to be reckoned with onstage.

Best Foot Forward, originally a 1941 Broadway musical, was a lighthearted, comic comedy about a young guy who falls in love with a showgirl while attending a college musical revue. While Minnelli did not play the lead in the show, her performance captivated both spectators and reviewers. She brought a young enthusiasm, charisma, and raw skill to the stage that set her apart from the other performers. The concert, although not a huge success, presented Liza with an excellent chance to hone her abilities, acquire the art of engaging an audience, and improve her stage presence.

Liza's debut Broadway performance demonstrated the charm and tenacity that would characterize her career. Despite its tiny size, this early job signaled the start of a long and famous association with Broadway and the theater industry. The production opened the door to other big chances, laying the groundwork for her future career.

**Flora, the Red Menace (1965)**

Liza Minnelli's career made a huge jump in 1965 when she was hired as the lead in Flora the Red Menace, a Broadway musical written by John Kander and lyricist Fred Ebb. The musical, which followed Flora, a young lady who aspires to be an artist but is confronted with the reality of life and love, was a fantastic showcase for Liza's skills. She portrayed the role with remarkable tenderness and emotional depth, making her not only approachable but also intriguing to spectators.

Liza's performance in Flora the Red Menace launched her famed relationship with Kander and Ebb, who went on to produce some of history's most memorable musicals, including Cabaret and Chicago. Liza's career took off with her performance in Flora the Red Menace, which got excellent reviews and won her the Tony Award for Best Actress in a Musical. Liza was 19 years old when she won this coveted prize, making her one of the youngest actors.

Her triumph in Flora the Red Menace not only catapulted her into the limelight but also revealed that she was capable of taking on complicated characters and bringing them to life in ways that few others could. This was the first of many situations in which Liza's emotional intelligence and depth as an actor shone through, establishing her as a versatile performer capable of playing humorous and serious parts.

**Tony Award Success and Theatre Legacy**
Liza's Tony Award triumph for Flora the Red Menace solidified her status as a rising Broadway star, but it was

just the beginning of her long and fruitful connection with the theater. Liza continued to make her imprint on the musical theatre scene in the years that followed, delivering ground-breaking performances.

Liza's career took off after winning the Tony Award, with other theatrical undertakings including her acclaimed 1974 concert Liza at the Winter Garden. This play, directed by the famous Bob Fosse, was a watershed point in Liza's career, establishing her as a real theatrical icon. The event included a spectacular combination of song, dance, and drama, and Liza's ability to captivate an audience with both her voice and her stage presence was highlighted like never before. Liza's achievement in the Winter Garden earned her a Special Tony Award in 1974, solidifying her stature in the Broadway world.

Throughout her career, Liza appeared in a number of important theatrical plays, including The Act (1977), which garnered her another Tony nomination. While the play was not as economically successful as Flora the Red Menace, Liza's performance once again showcased her mastery of the stage, especially as a fading diva attempting to recover her former grandeur. In the years that followed, she had success in more private settings, such as Liza at the Palace!, which earned her another Tony Award in 2009.

Beyond the honors, Liza's legacy in the theater is one of emotional depth, flexibility, and unrelenting dedication to her profession. Her contributions to musical theatre helped redefine the genre, and her performances continue to inspire generations of artists and spectators. Liza Minnelli's name is now associated with Broadway, and her work is an important part of the theater's rich history. Liza Minnelli's theatrical career, from her debut in Best Foot Forward to her breakthrough performances in Flora the Red Menace and beyond, demonstrates her persistent skill and enthusiasm for live performance.

# PART FOUR
## Transitioning to Music and Discography

# CHAPTER FOUR

## Liza Minnelli's Music

Liza Minnelli's flawless move from stage to music established her as a versatile and lasting celebrity. While she was previously recognized for her dramatic stage performances in musical theatre, her transition into music highlighted her extraordinary vocal range and distinct style. Liza's record is outstanding and broad, including a wide range of musical genres such as classic pop, musical theatre, disco, and even vocal jazz.

In 1964, she released her first album, Liza! Liza!, marking her first foray into the music industry. The CD included a combination of jazz and pop classics, demonstrating Liza's versatility. While the CD was favorably received, it was just the beginning of her journey into the music business.

Liza's music continued to change in the late 1960s and early 1970s, as she discovered her voice in a blend of dramatic, pop, and jazz songs. During this time, Liza Minnelli's recordings, including Liza Minnelli: Live at the London Palladium (1973) and Liza with a Z (1972), solidified her image as a powerful live performer and accomplished recording artist. These CDs showed her great vocal presence, amazing vocal control, and enthusiasm for singing. Her musical career would span many decades, with a succession of hit recordings that sealed her status as a pop and jazz star.

**Signature songs: "Cabaret" and "New York, New York"**

Liza Minnelli's name has been associated with some legendary tunes that continue to captivate listeners across the globe. Two of her best-known songs are "Cabaret" and "New York, New York."

"Cabaret" became Liza's hallmark song, inspired by the 1972 film of the same name. Liza's heartbreaking but vivacious delivery of the song as Sally Bowles became not just a career highlight, but also an anthem for a generation. The song's addictive melody, along with Liza's passionate delivery, made it an immediate hit, and it has been a highlight of her live appearances for decades. The Cabaret soundtrack, along with the film's critical acclaim, catapulted Liza to worldwide celebrity, and "Cabaret" became a rallying cry for anybody looking to transcend life's restrictions via self-expression and happiness.

Following the triumph of Cabaret, Liza's performance of "New York, New York" was another watershed event in her career. Originally composed for the 1977 film New York, New York, Liza's soaring vocals on this single entrenched it as a famous hymn for the city that never sleeps. Her version of the song, which was finally recorded and published as a single, has become associated with New York City, with its audacious proclamation of perseverance and hope. "New York, New York" is still one of Liza's most popular songs, often heard throughout her live performances and enjoyed by audiences all over the globe.

The popularity of these two legendary songs helped cement Liza Minnelli's reputation as one of her generation's greatest singers, and her ability to convey emotion and sincerity to each performance assured that these songs would transcend their original settings and take on new lives.

**Touring with Frank Sinatra and Sammy Davis Jr.**

Liza Minnelli's career took another dramatic turn in the late 1980s when she went on an amazing tour with two of music's most renowned figures: Frank Sinatra and Sammy Davis Jr. The tour, billed Frank, Liza & Sammy: The Ultimate Event, was a star-studded spectacle that combined Liza's remarkable skill with the proven grandeur of Sinatra and Davis.

The trio's concerts were a fusion of jazz, swing, and show songs, demonstrating the magic that could occur when three of the finest performers of the twentieth century got together on stage. The presentations were a celebration of traditional American music, and Liza, Sinatra, and Davis easily connected with the audience because of their common passion for performance and storytelling. Their synergy was evident, and each musician brought their distinct style to the stage.

The tour was not just a showcase of musical prowess, but also a demonstration of Liza's flexibility and ability to hold her own against two of the most legendary performers in history. She was able to show off her incredible singing ability while also enjoying the companionship and chemistry that made the trip so unforgettable. Liza's performance in Frank, Liza & Sammy cemented her reputation as a prominent figure in live performance and elevated her to the ranks of music's greatest names.

# PART FIVE
## Liza Minnelli's Film

# CHAPTER FIVE

## Film

Liza Minnelli's cinematic career started with her breakout performance in Alan J. Pakula's drama The Sterile Cuckoo (1969). Liza's portrayal as Pookie Adams, an eccentric, sensitive college student, at the age of 23, was a break from her theatrical beginnings and demonstrated her ability to play more subtle and complicated characters. This part was critical in establishing her as a genuine actor, rather than merely a theatrical performer.

Liza's depiction of Pookie was both sensitive and compelling, adding a distinct layer of weirdness and complexity to the character. Her performance received significant praise, earning her an Academy Award nomination for Best Actress. Though she did not win the prize, the acknowledgment was a huge step forward in her career, demonstrating that she was more than simply a musical star; she was a true film actor with a developing range and the capacity to dominate the screen. Liza Minnelli's cinematic career began perfectly with The Sterile Cuckoo, which demonstrated to Hollywood that she was a formidable force.

**Cabaret (1972): Winning the Oscar**

Liza Minnelli's most memorable and career-defining moment was her depiction of Sally Bowles in the 1972 film Cabaret. The film, directed by Bob Fosse, was an adaptation of the Broadway musical of the same name, which had previously been a success on stage. Liza's portrayal of the carefree, tormented, and ultimately tragic nightclub singer transformed both her career and the film business.

Cabaret was a breathtaking combination of song, drama, and dance, and Liza's depiction of Sally Bowles was nothing short of electrifying. The film's daring, innovative depiction of 1930s Berlin amid the emergence of the Nazi dictatorship captivated viewers with its challenging subjects and magnificent performances.

Liza's performance, in particular, was memorable. Her interpretation of the title song, "Cabaret," became a generational anthem, embodying the spirit of resistance and freedom in an uncertain time.

Liza Minnelli received the Academy Award for Best Actress for her role in Cabaret, firmly establishing her position in Hollywood history. She became just the second woman in history to win the prize for a musical performance, and her success demonstrated her ability to transcend conventional genre barriers. Liza's emotional depth and daring devotion to the part immortalized by Sally Bowles, and Cabaret is still regarded as one of the finest musical pictures of all time.

Liza won an Oscar, a BAFTA, and a Golden Globe for her performance in Cabaret, cementing her status as one of the best actors of her time. This picture was the pinnacle of her early cinematic career and paved the way for future accomplishments.

### Hollywood Career Highlights: Lucky Lady, Arthur, and More.

Liza Minnelli's cinematic career took off with the phenomenal success of Cabaret. She featured in a variety of distinct and significant films, demonstrating her flexibility and skill as an actor.

Lucky Lady (1975), a romantic comedy directed by Stanley Donen, was a noteworthy picture during this period. Liza played with Gene Hackman and Burt Reynolds in this humorous picture set during Prohibition. While the picture did not get much critical acclaim, Liza's charm and brilliance were evident. Her ability to hold her own among the two main guys demonstrated her rising stardom in Hollywood.

Liza's next significant success was the 1981 picture Arthur, in which she co-starred with Dudley Moore and John Gielgud. The film was a huge financial hit, and Liza's portrayal as Linda Marolla, a lady who falls in love with a rich and eccentric playboy, was hailed for its warmth and wit. Though Liza was once again positioned as the love interest, her depiction of Linda added a new dimension to a character who might have easily been overshadowed by the film's male stars' shenanigans. Arthur was a financial success, earning Liza another Golden Globe Award for her performance.

# PART SIX

## Early TV Appearances and Variety Shows

# CHAPTER SIX

## Liza's Early TV Appearances and Variety Shows

Liza established herself as one of the most compelling celebrities of her period by making appearances on a number of television programs in the years that followed. In addition to musical numbers, her television appearances included interviews and cameos that emphasized her charm, wit, and humor, solidifying her place as a well-liked public figure.

**Development of Arrests and Later Career Rebirth**
Liza Minnelli had a number of TV appearances in the 1970s and 1980s, but she didn't have a major comeback until the early 2000s. Her work on the highly regarded comedy Arrested Development (2003–2013) served as this, introducing her to a new audience and solidifying her standing as a versatile actor with a keen sense of humor.

In Arrested Development, Liza played Lucille Austero, a wealthy and eccentric member of the Bluth family's complex network of relationships. Although her role was initially intended to be a guest appearance, her performance was so well received that she was cast as a regular character, bringing humor and gravity to the show. Liza's portrayal of Lucille was a superb fit for the strange, absurd humor of the series, and her performance and timing made her one of the most memorable characters.

The ensemble cast, which featured Jason Bateman, Michael Cera, and Portia de Rossi, gained recognition for their ability to create witty, sharp banter, and Arrested Development was a critical success. Liza's portrayal of Lucille was unforgettable, and each scene she starred in showcased her comedic skills. Her work on Arrested Development was a turning point in her television career and made it simple for her to enter the comedy and television comedy genres. After decades of being linked to more somber and musical performances, fans were ecstatic to see Liza embrace her comedic side.

Liza Minnelli's adaptability and genius allowed her to keep up to date in the entertainment industry, as seen by the success of Arrested Development. Her transition from musical theater to film and then television showed off her extraordinary adaptability and solidified her status as one of the most beloved and enduring figures in entertainment.

Liza solidified her place in the pop culture landscape by continuing to make cameos on a variety of television programs after Arrested Development. By fusing her private life with her public persona, her roles in comedies like Will & Grace gave her legacy a new depth and gave her the chance to once again demonstrate her comedic timing.

Liza has starred in several TV movies, such as The Incident (2009), where she played a woman who had to deal with a group of unruly guests during a dinner party. Liza was able to maintain her reputation and keep her fans engaged with her work thanks to her low-key performances.

Although Liza has made fewer appearances on television in recent years, her impact on the medium has endured. From her groundbreaking musical specials to her legendary portrayal of Lucille Austero, Liza Minnelli's contributions to television have been as varied and extensive as her career in music and film.

Her work on television, especially in Arrested Development, demonstrated not only her timeless skill but also her capacity for fascinating self-reinvention, guaranteeing her stardom would endure in the entertainment industry.

# PART SEVEN

## Health Struggles and Impact on Performances

# CHAPTER SEVEN

## Liza's Health Struggles and Impact on Performances

In the 1980s and 1990s, Liza started to suffer from different health difficulties, including chronic diseases and complications that necessitated many operations and therapies. These issues were heightened by her persistent struggles with addiction and the physical toll of years of intense performances. In 1999, Liza made news when she had a series of procedures, including a hip replacement and knee surgery. Her physical health issues, compounded by a tough divorce from her fourth husband, David Gest, were a constant feature of the media coverage of her career.

Liza's health concerns required her to take a break from large-scale concerts for a while, but they did not reduce her desire to connect with her fans or continue performing. She was always motivated to return to the stage, and her ability to overcome her challenges and give strong, emotional performances only increased her fans' love and affection for her. Despite the failures, Liza's ability to persevere in the face of hardship became a significant aspect of her personal and professional story.

## Concerts at Carnegie Hall and Radio City Music Hall

Despite the difficulties she faced, Liza Minnelli's later career was defined by some of her most memorable and triumphant performances. In the 1980s, she staged several iconic concerts, the most notable of which were her performances at Carnegie Hall in 1979 and 1987. These performances were more than simply concerts; they were celebrations of Liza's exceptional skill and an expression of her intimate relationship with the audience. Carnegie Hall, one of the world's most prominent venues, has always played an important role in her creative career, and her return there demonstrated her enduring popularity.

Her 1987 Carnegie Hall performance was very impressive. The event was acclaimed as a huge success, demonstrating not just her remarkable vocal range but also her undying dedication to the art of performing. Liza's on-stage presence was nothing short of electrifying as she rehashed her iconic classics while also debuting new material to her devoted fans. Liza was able to connect with her audience in a personal and meaningful manner because of the intimacy of the venue, reinforcing her standing as one of her generation's finest performers.

Liza's appearances at Radio City Music Hall in 1991 and 1992 undoubtedly aided her subsequent career resurgence. These performances, part of a bigger tour, saw Liza return to the stage with newfound vigor. The concerts included stunning staging and lavish production numbers, evoking Liza's signature theatricality and elegance. Despite her continued health concerns, these performances were among the most successful of her career. They demonstrated her indomitable spirit and her ability to connect with her audience, even while enduring enormous personal hardships.

## Small Retrospective Performances and Intimate Appearances

Liza's health issues persisted throughout the 2000s, so she moved her emphasis to smaller, more intimate performances rather than large-scale concerts. These brief retrospective concerts enabled her to maintain contact with her followers while more successfully managing her health. In the years after her surgeries and personal problems, Liza performed in more intimate settings, allowing her to connect with her audience without the physical constraints of a huge tour or large performance venue.

One of her most memorable performances at this time was Liza at the Palace! in 2009. This was a more modest and stripped-down presentation than her previous bigger performances, but it still demonstrated her incredible ability and stage presence. The event, which took place at the Palace Theatre on Broadway, was both a celebration of Liza's career and a return to her theatrical origins. Fans were moved as they saw Liza reminisce on her illustrious career while still demonstrating her exceptional singing talents.

Liza at the Palace!'s popularity helped cement her reputation as one of the most adored and renowned artists of her day. Despite the health challenges that had kept her away from the stage for some time, she demonstrated that her legacy was far from gone. The play earned her a Special Tony Award, acknowledging her ability to create a riveting performance despite emotional and physical challenges. It demonstrated her perseverance and passion for the art of performing.

# PART EIGHT
## Marriages and Family Life

# CHAPTER EIGHT

## Personal Life of Liza Minnelli

Liza Minnelli has been married four times, each representing a distinct period in her life, career, and personal development. Her partnerships have been high-profile, often attracting the attention of the public and media, thanks to her celebrity status and the cultural relevance of her familial heritage.

**Peter Allen (1967–1974)**

Liza's first marriage was to Peter Allen, an Australian singer and composer renowned for his flamboyant flair and musical abilities. The couple married in 1967, and their relationship was one of the most public in Liza's early life. Allen had a significant effect on Liza's early music career, assisting her development as a performer. He wrote many of Liza's songs, including "I Honestly Love You" and "Don't Cry Out Loud," which became successes.

However, their marriage was not without difficulties. Allen's issues with his sexuality, culminating in his coming out as homosexual, strained their relationship. Despite their mutual affection, the marriage dissolved in 1974, only a few years after Liza won an Oscar for her performance in Cabaret (1972). The divorce was cordial, and the two remained friends until Allen died in 1992. Liza subsequently remembered warmly their time together, recognizing the value of their creative collaboration.

### Jack Haley, Jr. (1974–1979)

Liza's second marriage was to Jack Haley Jr., a director, and producer who was the son of Jack Haley, Sr., the actor best known for portraying the Tin Man in The Wizard of Oz (1939), which featured Liza's mother, Judy Garland. The marriage started in 1974, barely a year after Liza's divorce from Peter Allen, and lasted five years.

Liza's marriage to Haley was one of her most intimate, with many facts of their time together buried in secrecy.

However, like her previous marriage, their relationship was tumultuous, and they divorced in 1979. Haley remained a famous person in Hollywood, but he and Liza did not maintain a close relationship after their divorce.

### Mark Gero (1979–1992)

Liza's third marriage was with artist Mark Gero, whom she married in 1979. The couple's relationship lasted 13 years until they divorced in 1992. Mark Gero was an artist and sculptor, and their marriage enabled Liza to live a more tranquil, private existence. During their time together, Liza concentrated on her profession and health, which had deteriorated in the years after her high-profile achievements. Gero was a constant presence in Liza's life throughout this time, but like with her previous marriages, the relationship ended in divorce.

Despite their split, Liza talked highly of Gero in later years, recalling how they were able to support each other professionally and psychologically. They remained friends after their divorce, and Gero was one of the few individuals who supported Liza at some of the most difficult times in her professional and personal life.

**David Gest (2002–2007)**

Liza's most notorious marriage was with David Gest, a British-American producer and television personality. The two married in 2002 in a highly publicized wedding attended by several celebrities, including Liza's longtime friend Michael Jackson. Their marriage, however, was marred by public scandals and claims of domestic abuse. The couple's divorce in 2007 was highly contentious, with both parties claiming abuse and mistreatment.

Despite the controversy surrounding their marriage, Liza and David remained on relatively good terms after their divorce. David Gest remained a constant in Liza's life, and she spoke about him in interviews with a mix of nostalgia and sadness following his death in 2016. Their marriage was turbulent, but it was also one of Liza's most prominent and widely discussed partnerships.

### Family Dynamics: Lorna Luft, Joey Luft, and Judy Garland's Legacy

Liza's relationship with her family, particularly her half-siblings Lorna Luft and Joey Luft, Judy Garland's children from her second marriage to director Vincente Minnelli, is an important aspect of her personal life. Liza and her siblings had a complicated connection with their mother, Judy Garland, whose addiction and mental health issues had a significant influence on their childhood.

### Lorna Luft & Joey Luft

Liza's elder half-sister, Lorna Luft, has also had a great career in the entertainment industry, notably in acting and singing. Despite their terrible family dynamics as children, the two sisters have maintained a tight friendship throughout the years. Lorna has always praised her sister's amazing skill and the fortitude Liza showed during her career. Lorna, who has also written about growing up in the shadow of Judy Garland, has always had a close connection with Liza, despite having

51

to negotiate the complications of their mother's influence.

Joey Luft, Liza's younger half-brother, has had a gentler life than Lorna and Liza. He has mostly remained out of the public glare, although he maintains tight relationships with his family, which includes Liza. Joey, like his sisters, grew up with the weight of Judy Garland's reputation and public expectations of what it meant to be a member of the Garland family.

**The Legacy of Judy Garland**

Judy Garland's legacy hangs enormous over Liza Minnelli's life. As the daughter of one of Hollywood's most renowned performers, Liza was both burdened and inspired by the memories of her mother. Judy's battles with addiction, mental health concerns, and chaotic relationships had a long-lasting impact on her children, particularly Liza. However, despite Judy's issues, Liza has continuously talked about the love and respect she had for her mother, understanding the complexities of their connection.

Liza has frequently reflected in interviews on the lessons she learned from Judy Garland, both in terms of her mother's incredible work ethic and the pitfalls of celebrity. Liza's rise to fame, struggles with addiction, and eventual self-empowerment have all been influenced by Judy Garland's life lessons—both triumphs and tragedies.

The influence of Judy Garland's legacy on Liza Minnelli is undeniable. It has influenced Liza's approach to her career, public image, and personal relationships. While Liza has had to forge her path in the limelight, she has always carried her mother's memory and legacy with her, serving as both an inspiration and a reminder of the difficulties of living in public view.

# PART NINE

## Contributions to Charities and Causes

# CHAPTER NINE

## Philanthropy

Liza Minnelli's philanthropic efforts encompass a wide range of causes, from healthcare to arts funding, reflecting her diverse interests and deep desire to help those in need. She has actively participated in countless benefit concerts, charity events, and fundraising drives throughout the years, generating millions of dollars for a variety of organizations.

One of her key goals has been to assist health-related activities, especially those relating to the AIDS pandemic. The AIDS pandemic decimated relatives and friends throughout the 1980s and 1990s, and Liza, a long-time LGBTQ champion, worked relentlessly to raise awareness and cash for research. She appeared in several high-profile AIDS-related events, including benefit concerts and television charity programs. Liza's engagement in such activities was part of her continued commitment to improving the lives of individuals afflicted by the condition and lowering the stigma associated with it.

Liza has funded children's hospitals, medical research institutions, and programs that provide shelter and food to the destitute. Her involvement in such projects, which typically take the shape of benefit concerts or public appearances, has helped to raise awareness and much-needed funding. Liza Minnelli's contributions demonstrate a deep concern for the well-being of others, using her celebrity to shine a light on issues that are frequently overlooked by the mainstream.

**Her Support of the LGBTQ Community**

Liza Minnelli has long been a revered figure in the LGBTQ community, both as a performer and ally. Her honesty, generosity, and unabashed attitude to being herself have won over generations of LGBTQ people, and she has tirelessly campaigned for their rights and well-being. Liza's connection to the community is strong, with many fans viewing her as an icon not only for her talent but also for her authenticity and the warmth with which she welcomes all people, regardless of sexual orientation.

Liza has advocated for the LGBTQ community both personally and publicly. She has been an active supporter of homosexual rights since the 1970s, presenting at charity concerts and attending LGBTQ pride celebrations. One of her most remarkable acts of advocacy occurred in 1979 when she gave a well-publicized performance at New York City's renowned Carnegie Hall. This performance, which was widely acclaimed by the LGBTQ community, was a watershed moment in which Liza utilized her position to advocate for inclusiveness and acceptance. Over the years, she has often spoken out in favor of homosexual rights, including same-sex marriage and other LGBTQ rights.

Perhaps most famously, Liza Minnelli has long been a prominent supporter of the struggle against discrimination, especially homophobia and the stigma associated with HIV/AIDS. She has collaborated with groups such as the Human Rights Campaign and the Trevor Project, providing her name and resources to those committed to the well-being of LGBTQ people. Her activism in this area was particularly important during the 1980s and 1990s when the HIV/AIDS epidemic hit and many of the LGBTQ population experienced both health issues and widespread prejudice.

Liza has also continuously emphasized the significance of accepting one's uniqueness and living truthfully. Her performances, which are typically full of fire, passion, and an unabashed sense of self, have inspired numerous LGBTQ people who are grappling with their own identities. Her personification of personal freedom, along with her incredible skill, has made her an icon for a group that has long sought acceptance and prominence.

## Liza's Iconic Status among the LGBTQ Community

Liza Minnelli's place as a lesbian icon is firmly cemented, partially owing to her dedication to both her talent and her community. Her performances in films like Cabaret (1972) and New York, New York (1977) demonstrated her strong and unashamed personality, which appealed to LGBTQ audiences. But it wasn't simply her on-screen representations of strong, distinct characters that won her over the LGBTQ community. Her real-life acts, both on and off stage, have also helped her maintain her status as one of the community's most popular characters.

Her legendary performance of "New York, New York," both in the film and live, became an anthem for many members of the LGBTQ community. The lyrics—"If I can make it there, I'll make it anywhere"—spoke to the tenacity and resolve felt by so many LGBTQ folks, who regularly confront persecution and struggle. Over the years, this song, together with Liza's unwavering attitude, has represented the force of perseverance and the pursuit of one's aspirations, no matter the obstacles.

Liza's openness to openly recognize her particular affinity with her LGBTQ fans helped to solidify their friendship. At different periods in her career, she has referred to her LGBTQ admirers as "family," acknowledging their shared devotion. In addition to her music and performances, her work as a humanitarian and advocate has further strengthened this unique bond.

**An Enduring Legacy of Compassion and Advocacy**

Liza Minnelli's humanitarian legacy is characterized by compassion, dedication, and an unwavering desire to assist people in need. Her donations to many organizations and causes have affected countless lives, but her unflinching support for the LGBTQ community may have had the most long-term influence. Liza has become more than simply a musician thanks to her activism, public remarks, and personal engagement in philanthropic activities; she has become a light of hope and encouragement for many individuals who often feel excluded or overlooked.

Liza Minnelli's dedication to utilizing her celebrity for good has remained one of her most distinguishing characteristics throughout her career. Liza Minnelli's charitable endeavors, whether supporting causes such as

HIV/AIDS research or advocating for LGBTQ rights, have shown that her influence extends well beyond the stage, film set, or concert hall. She continues to inspire and encourage others via her philanthropic efforts, ensuring that her legacy is recognized not just for her exceptional talent, but also for her commitment to making the world a better place for everyone.

## CONCLUSION

Liza Minnelli's career in music, cinema, and theater is nothing short of legendary, and her impact extends well beyond her stunning performances. Liza has captivated the world with her incredible skill, perseverance, and heart, from her early years as the daughter of two show business titans to her rise to prominence as a renowned singer and vocal philanthropist. Her legacy, woven from a tapestry of spectacular performances, revolutionary achievements, and an unshakable dedication to justice, particularly for the LGBTQ community, will last for years.

Liza's narrative is more than simply a celebrity biography; it's the story of a woman who dared to live by herself, never shying away from obstacles and utilizing her position to inspire others. Whether in the spotlight or behind the scenes, Liza Minnelli's influence is felt in ways that words alone cannot adequately express. Her life exemplifies the strength of passion, tenacity, and the unwavering spirit of a real performer. And when we look back on her career, it's evident that Liza Minnelli will always be a bright example of the power of art and the unbreakable fortitude of the human spirit.